YOUR KNOWLEDGE HAS VALUE

Tim Pfefferle

Aus der Reihe: e-fellows.net stipendiaten-wissen

e-fellows.net (Hrsg.)

Band 782

Power and the Xingú: Policy Proposals on the Construction of the Belo Monte Dam

GRIN Verlag

Bibliografische Information der Deutschen Nationalbibliothek:

Die Deutsche Bibliothek verzeichnet diese Publikation in der Deutschen National-
bibliografie; detaillierte bibliografische Daten sind im Internet über http://dnb.d-
nb.de/ abrufbar.

Imprint:

Copyright © 2012 GRIN Verlag GmbH
Druck und Bindung: Books on Demand GmbH, Norderstedt Germany
ISBN: 978-3-656-49279-5

This book at GRIN:

http://www.grin.com/en/e-book/232450/power-and-the-xingu-policy-proposals-on-
the-construction-of-the-belo-monte

GRIN - Your knowledge has value

Der GRIN Verlag publiziert seit 1998 wissenschaftliche Arbeiten von Studenten, Hochschullehrern und anderen Akademikern als eBook und gedrucktes Buch. Die Verlagswebsite www.grin.com ist die ideale Plattform zur Veröffentlichung von Hausarbeiten, Abschlussarbeiten, wissenschaftlichen Aufsätzen, Dissertationen und Fachbüchern.

Visit us on the internet:

http://www.grin.com/

http://www.facebook.com/grincom

http://www.twitter.com/grin_com

TIM PFEFFERLE

Power and the Xingú:

Policy Proposals on the Construction of the Belo Monte Dam

INS 380B

November 29, 2012

Introduction

This policy proposal will assess the viability of the planned construction of the large hydroelectric dam in the state of Pará in northern Brazil. It will be outlined that, politically, ecologically, as well as economically, the Belo Monte dam will not yield the desired results and will therefore lead to avoidable disappointments. Thus, an alternative mix of energy sources will be proposed and contrasted with the dam project.

Since the mid-1970s, various Brazilian governments have looked at the possibilities of harnessing the vast hydroelectric potential provided by the various streams of the Amazon. The most controversial of these is the proposed Belo Monte dam on the Xingú river in the state of Pará, which according to some estimates could add an equivalent of ten percent of Brazil's energy production to the grid (Power, April 22, 2010). Given Brazils meteoric rise in terms of economic growth, poverty alleviation and reduction of inequality, energy is one of the key issues the country has to deal with to secure the gains that have been made. As noted by Kemmler and Spreng, human activity is closely related to the use of energy (2007: 2466). Furthermore, it is an essential factor of social inclusion, and its absence can lead to energy poverty (Pereira Jr. et al., 2008: 76).

However, the construction of the dam has been questioned in terms of its negative impact on the environment as well as its social ramifications with regard to the possible displacement of indigenous communities. The larger issue which encapsulates these two problems is the way the dam project exposes the challenges facing Brazil's institutional structure. On the one hand, it calls into question how the Brazilian government approaches the reconciliation between economic growth and environmental protection. On the other, it exposes a general problem within democratic theory: the status of minorities within a representative democracy.

Policy Options

Option A: Extensive Dam Construction

In the early 2000s, Brazil experienced extended periods of electricity shortages and blackouts (Lerner, 2010). Given Brazil's status as an emerging economy, growing energy demand will be one of the main challenges to face the country. According to figures provided by Geller et al., energy use per capita increased by 60 percent between 1975 and 2000 (2004: 1438). Tolmasquim et al. estimate that, by 2030, per capita energy use will have grown by more than 50 percent (2007: 4). Thus, as pointed out by The Economist, "investing in more power generation is essential" (Power, March 22, 2010). Currently, hydroelectric power accounts for more than 75 percent of the electricity produced in Brazil (Energy, December 5, 2011). With regard to the future capacity of hydroelectricity, Perreira et al. argue that "about 70% of the hydraulic potential to be taken advantage of is in Amazonia and in the Cerrado" (2008: 81).

This is the context in which the administrations of former president Lula da Silva and current president Rousseff have argued for the construction of the Belo Monte Dam. According to *The Economist*, it would add ten percent to the existing generating capacity (March 24, 2010), while bringing electricity to an estimated 23 million homes (Lerner, 2010). Fearnside concedes that the Belo Monte site is very advantageous due to its physical features (2006: 23). Apart from the Belo Monte dam, Brazil's 2011-2020 energy-expansion plan adds an additional 48 large dams (Fearnside, 2012: 1).

Thus, the trajectory is clear. The rationale behind the construction of large-scale dam projects is the concern for sustained economic growth, which will to depend to a significant degree on the consolidation of energy supply. Thus, Policy Option A will involve the construction of the Belo Monte Dam itself, but moreover will also include the construction of further dams upstream to ensure the economic viability of Belo Monte itself. According to Turner, up to six slightly smaller dams are necessary to make the Belo Monte Dam economically profitable within a reasonable timeframe (2011: 3). Nevertheless, in a discussion round on *Al-Jazeera*, Ken Green has pointed out that, in general, new constructions are more cost-effective than the maintenance of existing energy infrastructure (Inside, February 1, 2012). By most estimates, the dam will cost the Brazilian state at least eleven billion US dollars (Power, March 24, 2010).

The construction of the dam will be embedded within the general framework of a retention of the current energy mix, which relies to a significant extent on fossil fuels and hydroelectric power. With the construction of further dams, hydropower will be consolidated as Brazil's dominant source of electricity. Thus, in a nutshell, Policy Option A represents the continuation of Brazil's current energy policy.

Policy Option B: Belo Monte as Single Site

Goodland's definition of sustainability defines the term such that "environmental and social damage has been prevented or offset such that net residual impacts are insignificant" (2001: 1426), emphasizing that it is not only a "continuation of power output" (Ibid). Thus, while the construction of the Belo Monte Dam may require the addition of further dams upstream to ensure the economic viability of the project, the social and environmental impacts need to be fully accounted for. The basic struggle contained within the issue raised by Belo Monte is the trade-offs between economic development, or what is perceived as such, and the long-term damage created in environmental and social terms.

The Amazonian area of the Xingú has so far been left undisturbed for the most part. Thus, Turner describes it as "the most diverse ecosystem in Brazilian Amazonia" (2006: 2). The construction of the dams as outlined in Policy Option A could lead to the extinction of a significant number of species of fish in the Xingú and a general loss of biodiversity (Inside, February 1, 2012). Moreover, hydroelectric dams can be found to produce more greenhouse gas emissions than equivalent fossil fuel power plants in the short to medium terms, given that they emit high levels of methane, a particularly intense gas (Fearnside, Pueyo, 2012: 384). However, Barrionuevo maintains that if Belo Monte fails to materialize Brazil will be forced to rely on more harmful ways of electricity generation (April 17, 2010: A7). Nevertheless, the combination of the destructive potential of the dam and the potential absence of emissions savings point to severe environmental problems associated with it.

Hence, Policy Option B will try to contain the destructive potential entailed by the dam, which would be multiplied in the case of the realization of Policy Option A. Thus, while facing the possibility that the construction of the Belo Monte Dam as a single entity might entail economic inviability, the huge environmental costs need to be accounted for. Therefore, this option accepts the possibility that the dam will become a white elephant. However, construction has started now and a lot of time and financial resources have been poured into the project. According to a Folha de Sao Paulo public opinion survey, around 52 percent of

3

the population supported the dam project as recently as April of 2010 (Tug of War, February 28, 2011). Therefore, in political terms, the failure to go ahead with the project might entail a loss of face for President Dilma Rousseff, who sponsored the dam specifically when she was Chief of Staff in the Lula administration (Turner, 2011: 2). Moreover, Belo Monte is the centerpiece of Brazil's Project for Accelerated Development introduced under President Lula da Silva (Ibid). Therefore, the current administration will be under pressure to show coherence and at least build the Belo Monte site.

However, to appease the critics on both sides, additional measures have to be taken. Both business and environmentalists will not be satisfied by this compromise alone. Thus, President Dilma would need to push both natural gas production and encourage the development of true renewable energy sources. The construction of Belo Monte would therefore be embedded in a more comprehensive energy strategy.

Policy Option C: Energy Policy without Belo Monte

Having investigated the economic and environmental dimensions of the dam project, what has so far not been taken into account is the effect its construction will have in social terms, as well as the institutional ramifications implied by the process through which the proposal was ratified. Thus, Policy Option C will argue for the complete abandonment of the Belo Monte project, taking into consideration the questionable economic benefits outlined above, the serious environmental consequences which have been discussed, as well as the social and institutional impacts to be delineated shortly.

According to Turner, the Brazilian constitution of 1988 mandates that "indigenous communities be consulted in advance" (2011: 2) on projects such as this large scale hydroelectric construction. However, this has failed to happen in a satisfying way. The indigenous communities in the relevant area of the Xingú were found not to be "directly impacted" in an environmental study which was carried out (Fearnside, 2012: 2). This conclusion was apparently arrived at on the basis that they did not live in the immediate vicinity of the dam structures themselves. However, it does not take much imagination to contemplate the damage that might be done to these communities, which will undoubtedly be affected by the general loss in biodiversity, given their primary occupation as fishermen.

It is estimated that the displaced population will amount to at least 12000 people, with some estimates ranging up to 320000 people, taking into consideration the wider implications the dam could potentially entail (Lerner, July 1, 2010). According to Fearnside, they comprise 37 ethnicities (2006: 16). Thus, the question is what happens to those communities which do get displaced. So far, Brazil's government has not allocated sufficient land for displaced communities (Lerner, July 1, 2010). This is of course a challenge given the problem of uprooting indigenous peoples and establishing them in a different locale. Furthermore, the indigenous communities have not had access to a social and environmental impact assessment study in their languages, which effectively disempowers them and excludes them from participating effectively in the consultation process (Brazil, June 2, 2011). Lastly, concrete measures would have to be taken to prevent the potential spread of diseases among the indigenous communities as a result of the construction of the dam. All of these factors point to a possible disaster for the indigenous population affected by the Belo Monte Dam. Thus, a report commissioned by the International Labor Organization found that there "is no evidence that [the consultation procedures] enabled the Indigenous Peoples to take part effectively in determining their priorities" (quoted in Fraser, March 10, 2012)

The second dimension which casts serious doubts about the viability of the project is the character of Brazil's institutional processes through which the construction of the dam has been pushed through. While Brazil's own Ministry of Public Works denounced the project as "illegal and in violation of the constitution (Turner, 2011: 3), presidents Lula da Silva and Rousseff have been impervious to most points of criticism. The basic problem is outlined by Barrionuevo: "[Brazil] has struggled to find a balance between the push to develop and the demand to protect the delicate ecosystems and indigenous peoples of the Amazon" (April 17, 2010: A7). However, within this context, the Belo Monte project has showcased the institutional problems which exist in Brazil's environmental licensing system. Turner notes the "blatant corruption of the legal system by political pressure from the government (2006: 4), which is echoed by Fearnside (2006: 18). Hochstetler and Keck find that in general, the judiciary supports powerful actors over powerless actors when it comes to environmental questions (2007: 148). Thus, the head of Brazil's environmental agency was forced to resign as a result of his criticism of the project (Fearnside, 2012: 3). Moreover, the approval for the final go-ahead for the project in 2005 was pushed through the Senate in less than 48 hours (Ibid). Given the project's magnitude, this is alarming. Subsequently, three court injunctions were struck down to protect the construction of the dam (Lerner, 2010).

Therefore, Picq has suggested that the policies followed under the Lula and Dilma administrations have resembled those implemented by the military regimes of the 1970s (May

17, 2012). Brazil has also disrespected its regional and international commitments to various organizations. These include the Inter-American Commission on Human Rights, the International Labor Organization and the Organization of American States (Ibid). Hence, both in domestic as well as international terms, the project's hushed and obscure approval casts doubt on Brazil's institutional ability to handle environmental policy. This is reflected in other areas as well, most notably with regard to deforestation (Compromise, June 2, 2012). This suggests that the successful construction of the Belo Monte site would represent a further breakdown of Brazil's institutional system. Therefore, Fearnside concludes that "the main issue raised by the Belo Monte Dam is more profound than the direct impacts at the reservoir site; it is the system in which dam building decisions take place" (2006: 23). What rights do minorities have in Brazil, and specifically with regard to indigenous peoples? How can Brazil ensure that democratic ideas can be squared with its idea of development? These are the wider issues raised by the Belo Monte project.

Given the doubts about the viability of the dam site, Option C proposes a construction stop. This will require a more wholesale reform of the energy sector. Brazil will need to capitalize on its significant renewable energy potential in terms of wind, solar and biofuel energy (Geller et al., 2004; 1438). To ensure energy security, natural gas production should be encouraged. Moreover, since hydropower will still be an important component of the energy mix, there is a need for alternative engineering solutions (Pereira et al., 2008: 81). This will mean smaller dam sites in viable locations. Lastly, Brazil needs to make efforts to slow down its medium to long-term growth in aggregate energy demand. Thus, inefficiencies in industrial processes as well as the transportation sector will need to be reduced. In terms of emissions, McKinsey & Company identify agriculture and deforestation as the main areas which need to be tackled (March 2009: 7).

There is a wide range of political entrepreneurs who can advocate this position. Pro-Indigenous NGOs such as *Cultural Survival* and the *Missionary Indigenous Council* have been outspoken opponents of the project. There are a number of Non-Indigenous NGOs as well, such as the *Movement of Dam-Affected People*. Environmental NGOs will naturally play a part, which includes the *International Rivers Network* and *Environmental Defense*. Within government, opponents of the dam can be found as well, most notably the Ministry of the Environment and the *Brazilian Institute of the Environment and Renewable Natural Resources*. Academic entities which have been outspoken include the *University of Sao Paulo* and the *National Institute for Research in the Amazon*. The Chair of the Senate's environmental Committee, Ricardo Tripoli, a member of the social democratic PSDB has also been an opponent of Belo Monte and has had some success advocating against it in Congress (Belo Monte, April 28, 2010)

Conclusion

This policy proposal argues that the benefits derived from the Belo Monte dam project do not outweigh the environmental and social costs associated with it. Combined with the prospect that Brazil's institutional framework has not been able to handle this project, these profound problems mean that the project should be stopped. In its place, a reformed energy strategy has been proposed, which will include more natural gas, smaller dams, as well as increased renewable energy production. Therefore, Belo Monte should be abandoned.

Sources

Barrionuevo, A., "Amazon Dam Project Pits Economic Benefit Against Protection of Indigenous Lands," *The New York Times,* April 17, 2010, p. A7.

"Brazil Urged to Suspend Belo Monte Dam Project," *Amnesty International*, June 2, 2011, http://www.amnesty.org/en/news-and-updates/brazil-urged-suspend-belo-monte-dam-project-2011-06-02, accessed November 29, 2012.

Fearnside, P. M., "Dams in the Amazon: Belo Monte and Brazil's Hydroelectric Development of the Xingu River Basin," *Environmental Management* Vol. 38, No. 1 (2006), pp. 16-27.

Fearnside, P. M., "Belo Monte Dam: A Spearhead for Brazil's Dam-Building Attack on Amazonia?," *Global Water Forum*, GWF Discussion Paper 1210, March 2012, http://www.globalwaterforum.org/2012/03/19/belo-monte-dam-a-spearhead-for-brazils-dam-building-attack-on-amazonia/, accessed November 29, 2012.

Fearnside, P. M., Pueyo, S., "Greenhouse-Gas Emissions from Tropical Dams," *Nature Climate Change* Vol. 2 (2012), pp. 382-384

Fraser, B., "International Labor Organization Concerned with Lack of Indigenous Input on Belo Monte," *Amazon Watch*, March 10, 2012, http://amazonwatch.org/news/2012/0310-international-labor-organization-concerned-with-lack-of-indigenous-input-on-belo-monte, accessed November 29, 2012.

Geller et al., "Policies for Advancing Energy Efficiency and Renewable Energy Use in Brazil," *Energy Policy* Vol. 32 (2004), pp. 1437-1450.

Goodland, R. J. A., "The Future of Big Dams," *Water and Development* Vol. 1 (2001), pp. 1419-1432.

Hochstetler, K., Keck, M. E., *Greening Brazil: Environmental Activism in State and Society* (Durham: Duke University Press, 2007).

"Inside Story Americas: The Real Cost of Brazil's Dam," *Al Jazeera*, February 1, 2012, http://www.aljazeera.com/programmes/insidestoryamericas/2012/02/201221111814807201.html, accessed November 29, 2012.

Kemmler, A., Spreng, D., "Energy Indicators for Tracking Sustainability in Developing Countries," *Energy Policy* Vol. 35 (2007), pp. 2466-2480.

Lerner, J., "Belo Monte Dam: The Costs of Development in Brazil," *Center for Strategic & International Studies*, July 1, 2012, http://csis.org/blog/belo-monte-dam-costs-development-brazil, accessed November 29, 2012.

"Pathways to a Low-Carbon Economy for Brazil," *McKinsey & Company* (São Paulo: McKinsey & Company, March 2009).

Pereira et al., "Energy in Brazil: Toward Sustainable Development?," *Energy Policy* Vol. 36 (2008), pp. 73-83.

Picq, M., "Belo Monte: Brazil's Damned Democracy," *Al Jazeera,* May 17, 2012, http://www.aljazeera.com/indepth/opinion/2012/05/2012515144822206262.html, accessed November 29, 2012.

"Power and the Xingu; Energy in Brazil," *The Economist*, April 22, 2010, http://www.economist.com/node/15954573, accessed November 2012.

Tolmasquim et al., Visão Prospectiva da Matriz Energética Brasileira: Energizando o desenvolvimento sustentável do país, *Revista Brasileira de Energia* Vol. 13, No. 1, pp. 1-19.

Tripoli, R., "Belo Monte: Comissão de Meio Ambiente aprova requerimento de Tripoli," April 28, 2010, http://www.ricardotripoli.com.br/?p=117, accessed November 29, 2012.

"Tug of War over Belo Monte Dam," *Latin Business Chronicle*, February 28, 2011, http://www.latinbusinesschronicle.com/app/article.aspx?id=4789, accessed November 29, 2012.

Turner, T., "The Long Struggle over the Xingú Dams Comes to a Climax at Belo Monte," *Synthesis/Regeneration* Vol. 54 (2011), pp. 2-4.